Regional Movie Ministries

Kingdom Building through Networking, Faith, & Film

Rich Gerberding

Front Cover Design: Michael Anthony Noel

Published by Pray & Post Publishing,
14721 N Grandview Dr, Chillicothe IL 61523

ISBN:
978-0-9886427-0-6

DEDICATION

Dedicated to the countless people involved in all areas of Christian films, from funding to shooting, acting to editing, distributing to promoting.

May we all see the day when the word "surprise" is no longer used to describe the latest successful Christian film!

ACKNOWLEDGMENTS

Special thanks to my wife April, who has put up with me through the times where ministry slips from my "second full time job" (smile) to my "second full time job" (no smile). I can't imagine life without you.

To my son Jordan, a huge blessing whom I am proud to say is also my brother-in-Christ and partner in ministry. I can't wait to see what great things God does in and through your life.

To the Men of AIM Leadership Team - Jim Culver and Steve Crawford. Thanks for your support, ideas, and honest feedback. For too long this ministry rested on one set of shoulders, and I'm thankful for your faithfulness and passion for all aspects this ministry and helping me see when I am aiming too high - or too low.

CONTENTS

ENDORSEMENTS

The Regional Movie Ministries handbook is a fantastic tool for those interested in supporting faith-based films in a BIG way. I highly encourage anyone who wants to make a difference with Christian films to read this handbook and I look forward to sharing it with our many Movie to Movement Theater Captains!

> \- Josef Lipp, National Director, Movie to Movement
> www.movietomovement.com

If you are making a Christian movie, it is imperative that you take the time to read, study, and implement the suggestions within. Don't miss this opportunity to connect with Regional Movie Ministries.

> \- Roger & Annelie Rudlaff, Christian Film Database (CFDb)
> www.christianfilmdatabase.com

With the growth of Christian films, there is an increasing need to spread the word. Regional Movie Ministries has tapped into a way to build "grassroots awareness" of Christian films in their own region and are encouraging others to do the same. Anyone who cares about Christian movies should read this book.

> \- Cheryl Ariaz Wicker, film producer, host of Christian Movie Connect
> www.ChristianMovieConnect.com

If there were more people like Rich Gerberding around the country, faith-based films would be doing twice the box office they are now. His methods simply work, and distributors would be wise to not only use him for their films, but learn from him.

> \- Dallas Jenkins, Jenkins Entertainment
> Director, *What If...* (2010)

Rich Gerberding & the Heart of Illinois Christian Movie Central are a key reason Christian films "Play in Peoria." They have built a strategy to build momentum from film to film. I wish we had hundreds of groups around the country like them as we would really make an impact on our society. -

> \- Rich Christiano, www.Christianmovies.com
> Director, *The Secrets of Jonathan Sperry* (2009), *A Matter of Faith* (2014)

1 MOVIE OR MINISTRY?

"Why don't they make more movies like this?" It's heard as the lights come up following any well-made Christian movie. In the past, I'd simply smile or even nod in agreement, but over the last couple years, a new boldness has taken root. Here's a conversation I had following *COURAGEOUS* in the fall of 2011, when someone asked me...

"Why don't they make more movies like that?"

"Well, what did you think of *Seven Days in Utopia?*"

"When was that?"

"Did you see *Soul Surfer?*"

"No — but I did hear it was good."

"How about *The Grace Card?*"

"Um, no."

"It sounds like more films like this are being made, but you're not aware of or supporting many of them."

"I had no idea. I just didn't know."

We ended up discussing Christian films for about 10 minutes, including our efforts at Men of AIM (Action, Integrity, Maturity) to build grassroots awareness and support of Christian films through the Heart of Illinois Christian Movie Central.

Over the last several years, the writing, acting, and cinematography of Christian films have greatly improved, but they still struggle to compete in building awareness for the films, and in promotional budgets.

Sherwood Pictures, a ministry of Sherwood Baptist Church in Albany, Georgia, has been the best known source of Christian films in recent years. They took a volunteer army to film *Flywheel* in 2003, with a dream of seeing it play at their local theater, then saw it expand to others in the region. Its success on a shoestring budget led to larger budgets, improved marketing, and growing successes with subsequent efforts *Facing the Giants*, *FIREPROOF*, and most recently, *COURAGEOUS*.

But is it really just about marketing budgets? We believe Sherwood's growth came from staying connected to their audience from film to film - a strategy that can be applied at the local or regional level for Christian films in general regardless of who produced a specific film.

Nearly every Christian film that is out, is coming soon, or might be made sets up a web page. The internet is a fantastic tool, and allows the potential to reach millions of *potential* fans. The hurdle, of course, is moving from potential to actual. Once a specific fan finds a particular website, they are encouraged to register for that film's mailing list, in order to get information ranging from filming updates, to behind the scenes pictures or videos, to great and fabulous prizes (well, maybe.)

There is NOTHING wrong with this, as it pertains to that specific film, but it results in lost momentum and duplicated efforts.

Let's say a low budget film, Film A, scratches their way to 5,000 people signed up for updates. A second film, Film B, starts with a strong base and works up to 90,000 fans on their mailing list.

There are now 95,000 people interested enough in Christian films to say, "I want more information - send me emails!"

Eventually a third lower budget movie is developed, (you guessed it, Film C) and invests blood, sweat, prayers, and tears into filming and editing. What are their first steps?

That's right - start a web page. Set up a mailing list. Building another audience - from zero. The 95,000 from films A & B have no awareness of Film C, so they now must visit a third site, register, and join another list.

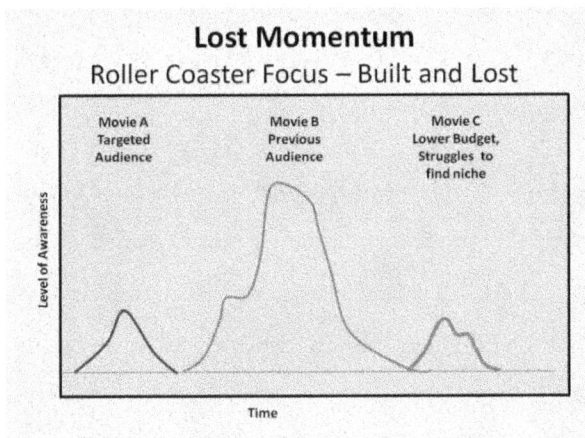

Lost Momentum
Roller Coaster Focus – Built and Lost

If the new filmmakers are fortunate, they may get an endorsement from a previous successful film team and get a boost. More likely, the typical Christian moviegoer misses out on Film C altogether, probably never heard of film A, and left Film B asking... you guessed it: "Why aren't there more Christian films?"

Is there another way?

Again, please don't take anything we are proposing or doing as a criticism against individual films, directors, or studios launching a web page, mailing list, or other resources to support their specific films. They absolutely should be doing this in today's social marketing driven world.

Our question is simple: How could we better harness the momentum of Films A and B in order to jump start Film C and other upcoming films?

When every movie starts over with a new website and email list, it can be confusing and frustrating for the fan who just wants to know what is out there. How much time can be spent simply searching "Christian Films" and "Christian movies 2014" and similar phrases? The answer? Quite a bit. (Trust me.)

To help with this, several national websites have come up which can help streamline this process of updating fans with news about that status of various films. These are great for learning about films in progress, who is starring in them, and when they are expected to come out to theaters or direct to DVD.

A downside to these national websites, however, is simply the fact they are... national. Knowing about a film that is opening in 80 theaters next month doesn't help someone who can't justify the 600-mile one way trip to the nearest city playing the film. Show anyone enough films they won't be able to see until the DVD two years later and see how they react to your next "Breaking Update."

Regional Movie Ministries

What if instead of a narrow focus ("Step right up for Film D – Here we go again!") or the wide (Visit our page and be overwhelmed with information on dozens of films which won't come anywhere near you."), we believe there is great potential for ministries willing to camp out between the two extremes, within a defined geographic area and actively engaging a growing audience over time.

Select an area large enough for a population to support films, but small enough people are willing to travel to the films. For a city, it might just be the city limits. For a more rural area, the coverage could be wider - since people from rural areas are more accustomed to driving longer distances for events - if they can see the value in doing so.

As a Regional Movie Ministry (RMM), the news being shared can be specific to the area. Rather than, "This film will come out in July," the RMM can share, "This film will come out in July at the following theaters." Depending on the geographic focus of the RMM, it may cover multiple cities/theaters.

Not every film plays in every market. This is, after all, still a business that requires the investors, producers, directors, and actors to put food on their table and meet some level of financial 'success' if they are to fund the next film. An RMM, is able to build an aware and supportive local market for Christian movies, as opposed to a specific film. When a large film with lots of national buzz comes to town, like *COURAGEOUS* or *Soul Surfer*, the regional ministry can connect to that audience.

A few months later, when a smaller film comes to the area, those who signed up at the blockbuster now hear about the new film, and the excuse of "I didn't know," goes right out the window.

Marketing is not a bad thing. In fact, it's a great thing, if done with integrity. Don't spin something as a Christian film because in scene 28 someone is holding a Bible. Oops, sorry, stepping off of that soap box for now. Better than marketing, however, is efficient marketing.

Who cares that 10,000,000 heard about your film if it cost you $200 million for the marketing and only 6,000 people who heard cared enough to show up? The challenge is to be both effective and efficient - to reach the most interested audience at the minimum cost.

Who is the key audience for a Christian film? How about the people who have gone and liked previous efforts? RMM's have the benefit of being the boots on the ground, who can talk to people at the movie theaters, the churches, the concerts, and other related gatherings in their region.

Marketing to the non-church crowd certainly has its place, but it can be very difficult to generate enough interest to get someone to the theater, but a personal invitation from a friend who does believe in the film may be enough to do the trick. So which audience do you market to - one stationary at best, resistant at worst - or one already leaning your direction?

Man in the Mirror developed a "No Man Left Behind" men's discipleship model for men's ministry. A key element of the model is the idea of "Create Value, Capture Momentum, Sustain Change."

The well funded and publicized film can be the big stadium event that creates value to get people focused and excited about a specific film, but the RMM is positioned to capture that interest and sustain the interest to and through the months ahead - building the potential impact, while decreasing the effort required to spread the word for upcoming films - now marketing to an already interested audience.

Rather than a roller coaster of effort, cost, and interest, an RMM facilitates growth in audience and interest throughout the cycle. Certainly a high-profile film with a couple well known stars can provide a more rapid boost, but in between films periodic updates allows recipients to forward or post updates to their friends, who can say, "Where did you hear about that? I'd like to sign up as well."

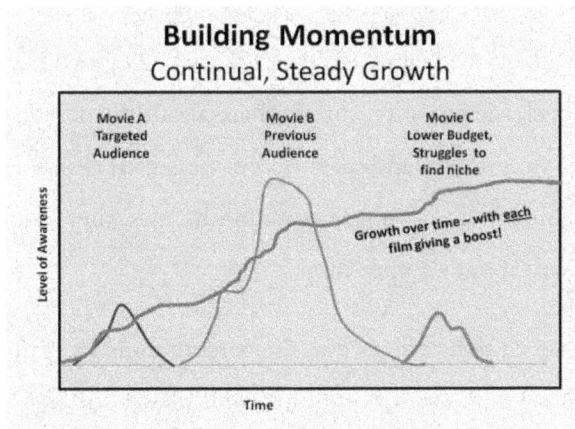

Building Momentum
Continual, Steady Growth

There is another key benefit to an RMM rather than a production studio effort. Because the RMM team is actually from the community, there is greater opportunity to build relationships and trust.

Imagine you're a pastor or secretary at a church, and someone you have never seen before walks into your office and says the following?

"Hey - there is a fantastic new movie coming out next month that you simply must get everyone in your congregation to see. I want you to play the trailer for every service, meeting, and opportunity for the next 3 weeks, pass out bulletin inserts and bookmarks at every opportunity, and read this scripted endorsement for a film you haven't even seen yet? Thanks. What? No? You won't? What's the matter, - don't you care about God's Kingdom?"

It takes time to build trust. I have sent a monthly e-mail newsletter for men's events in our region since 2003. Now, over a decade later, I still get the same hesitant questions when I contact a church or individual for permission to include and promote THEIR event, "How much does it cost? Why are you doing this?" It has gotten better, but it takes time to build that trust.

Now imagine if that same, enthusiastic, gung-ho, high energy person were to scale back the pressure, simply share about the movie, drop off information about the film and maybe a business card or something about their ministry and mission. Then, a few months later, they stop in and respectfully share about another film.

In time, the church realizes that the person/ministry is there to share what is happening in the area, and not to guilt, shame, or push them to do something against their will. The second, or fourth, or eighth movie shared might be one that triggers their ongoing interest - but not if the bridges are burned on the first visit by someone playing the "if your church really cared about the Kingdom you would do what I say you should do!" card.

So that's some theory and thoughts about this concept of a "Regional Movie Ministry." The question is, does it work in practice as well as theory?

All we can say for certain, is that it has worked here, and we put it in practice before even thinking about the idea's theoretical side.

The next chapter will review how we came to be part of the world of Christian movies, then most of the booklet is about sharing some of what we've learned. This is not meant to be an exhaustive tome on what to do step-by-step in five years because we already know it all. (We don't!)

We'd like to hear stories of people who decided to take this on before even finishing the book, learn with us, and teach us by sharing what you have learned. We want to build a network of regional movie ministries working together yet separate. Not led by a central directive, but doing what works in your region, but communicating with others so we can all learn and be more effective - together, and most importantly, in setting the stage (theater?) for maximizing the impact of Christian films for the Kingdom!

ACTION! Where in your life or ministry have you seen momentum lost - where a lot of work was spent and weeks (or days) later you realized an opportunity was lost? Record your thoughts on the next page.

Where (films, ministry, or elsewhere) do you want to see this change)?

2 IT HAS PLAYED IN PEORIA (SURELY YOU SAW THAT ONE COMING)

I used to hate Christian movies. I know, "hate" is a strong word, and if you are offended, I'm sorry that you were offended but the word fits, so I'm using it.

I'm not saying every film was terrible or that I harbor any dislike towards anyone who ever made a Christian film. I just did not care for the movies. As a non-Christian growing up I never saw one that impacted my worldview or thoughts about Jesus Christ. After becoming a Christian, the films might make me think about the choice I had made but I was not going to race out to share it with others - Christian or otherwise.

I share this to demonstrate I am one of the last people on the face of the earth I would have expected to be playing a small role in promoting Christian films. If you had told me in 2008 I would have never believed you. Come to think of it, that's a dangerous response because there are several other things over the years with that reaction, and at least three others also came true.

In the late spring of 2009, I received an email from a co-worker, Ed Stembridge, who had recently returned from the San Antonio Independent Christian Film Festival where his son, Chad, was a semi-finalist for an award. In San Antonio, director/producer Rich Christiano of 5&2 Pictures, screened his new film, *The Secrets of Jonathan Sperry*, and shared his desire to distribute the film through local sponsorships.

Rather than finding one Hollywood distributor to pay millions of dollars to get the movie in hundreds of theaters, Rich was looking for individuals, churches, or organizations in cities and towns across the country to say, "WE want to bring this film to our area." On the back end, if the film did well, a percentage of the funds usually returned to Hollywood film distributors stayed in the community with the local sponsors.

Ed expressed interest in bringing it to Peoria, and returned home prepared to cold call churches to raise the remaining funds. Before he started making the calls, another co-worker, Robert Christmas, recommended he contact me first. Robert and I had served together on the leadership team of two Promise Keepers events in Peoria, and he thought I might know of specific churches with interest.

Ed's email came late on a Friday, and I did not expect to hear anything until the next week from my non-committal, lukewarm reply to consider it, but not until I'd seen the film. Within an hour plans were set for Ed and his wife to come to our house to watch it with my family the next evening.

One scene sparked a decision to co-sponsor it in Peoria through Men of AIM (www.MenofAIM.org), our regional men's ministry. Jonathan Sperry (Gavin MacLeod) started a Bible study with some young boys in the neighborhood, and as that group of three expanded into a full living room of boys soaking up the wisdom of the Word of God through Jonathan Sperry.

We got on board, scheduled a few advanced screenings at local churches, and secured the remaining funding through the gracious (and surprise) support of WBNH 88.5FM, our local Moody radio station, after Station Manager Jim Huber came to a screening and talked to the station board the next day.

None of us had any idea what we were doing. We hosted three advanced screenings and invited whoever we could, repeatedly having to explain what an "Advanced Screening" was - a chance to see a film before it arrived in theaters, so people could share it from first-hand experience and not just the trailer. We posted flyers where we could and were thankful for numerous opportunities for interviews and discussions with WBNH. We also were able to schedule Rich Christiano for interviews on two other area Christian radio stations, 91.5FM WCIC and 1020AM WPEO.

When the film opened at Willow Knolls 14 in Peoria, we had no idea what to expect, but a strong opening weekend (far stronger than even we expected based on the positive but not heavily attended screenings) led to a strong second weekend. While we never were the top film at the theater, we were never beaten by a film that premiered before us. Films would open and beat us for a week or two, and then drop off dramatically, while our word of mouth kept us steady in what would become the film's third longest run in the nation, and the sixteenth highest grossing market.

One and done, we were finished. It was a lot of work, we'd

accumulated a fair number of people wanting updates on the film, but we had no intention of any ongoing Christian movie efforts.

Fast forward a few months. We had become more aware of several Christian films while promoting Jonathan Sperry, so we kept track of some. One, *To Save a Life*, was coming out in January, but not to Peoria. No problem, we'll wait for the DVD. Then, suddenly and without notice, it WAS in Peoria. My son and I went to see it on a Saturday of weekend two, joined by just six other people in the whole theater. Having learned how the movie theater process worked, I knew a second weekend with such a low turnout did not bode well, and started emails flying to let people know the film was here. I got a number of responses from disappointed youth leaders who had wanted to take their youth but didn't think it was coming to Peoria, and now had other plans.

On that Saturday, in a nearly empty theater, the seed for the Heart of Illinois Christian Movie Central was planted.

The following Thursday, *To Save a Life* left Peoria.

To be sure, we still didn't know what we were doing, but we did know what we did for *The Secrets of Jonathan Sperry* worked far better than what wasn't done for *To Save a Life*. We tossed together a quick logo, sketched out a few ideas of what we could do, and sent a note out to the mailing list inviting people who wanted to continue with movie updates to let us know. Most people did.

What we didn't know is whether anything we did would make a difference. In the spring of 2010, we got another call from Rich Christiano, who was involved through Pure Flix Entertainment with the distribution of a film titled *What If...*, directed and produced by Dallas Jenkins of Jenkins Entertainment.

Not knowing what to do, we did pretty much the same things as before. Advanced screenings, emails, and some radio interviews. My son and I visited Harvest Bible Chapel in Elgin, IL, for the movie premiere with him and the cast, then drove home and somehow got up for school and work the next day.

What If also got off to a strong start in Peoria. Again Peoria held the third longest run in the nation, and this time when our run ended our theater was ranked number seven in the nation. Peoria, for those of you who aren't familiar with our community, is not the #7 largest city in America, so I don't think anyone - ourselves, Rich Christiano, Dallas Jenkins, or anyone anticipated to see Peoria, Illinois in the top ten!

Since 2010, we have not directly sponsored any additional films, but this is where the credibility and relationships with churches and individual Christians builds. If we only promoted the two films which we "sponsored," then our involvement and support could have been written off as self interest.

The larger budget films (*Soul Surfer* from Sony, *COURAGEOUS* from Sherwood Pictures, and others) may contract with various marketing firms such as Lovell-Fairchild or Lifeway. These teams do a fantastic job promoting films and often host advanced leadership screenings in various cities - built up by contact lists from their past efforts. These are held in a movie theater (not in churches like ours were), and are very well done. These are events held for the specific movies, but because we're here to promote Christian films, we do all we can to connect church, business, and community leaders to these events as well – always respecting the host organization's authority and wishes.

ACTION! The movie ministry is an example where I responded quickly to an opportunity before me, but there have been many I missed due to fear, delay, or indecision.

Where is God calling you to step up and trust Him for something you never saw coming?

_____

_____

_____

_____

3 BRINGING IT HOME
(MAKING IT PLAY IN YOUR TOWN)

Mechanisms for bringing films to town vary, but the bottom line is still the bottom line. While Christian films have a higher purpose, it is still a business and they can't afford to repeatedly lose money, or funding future films will move from difficult to impossible.

Some films will have online competitions to determine where to come. *Beyond the Farthest Star* set up a "Bring It" page for cities to vote. *Hardflip* used a Facebook comment competition on their wall to measure support and select a city for a gathering with cast and professional skateboarders. Peoria won the *Hardflip* contest by a landslide.

Unfortunately, the *Hardflip* contest was for a single night's screening, not a theater run. We successfully lobbied for a theater run instead, but when no cast or skateboarders were available to kick-off the theater run, the online enthusiasm quickly fizzled. Always remember your goal is not to build online "likes" or potential audience - **you want (and need) people willing to back it up by actually coming out to the theaters - especially opening weekend!**

In any case, the people behind the film need to have confidence that if their film comes to town, it will do well. Not break even, but turn a strong profit. The simplest way to do this is to build a track record. They can see how past films have done in your town. You should have a feel of this as well, even if not with specific dollars.

One tool for this is the website www.boxofficemojo.com. Each week it tracks films' performance, including the gross sales for the weekend and since release, change in sales and theater counts, and per screen averages.

When a film opens nationwide and in your town, check each week to see how many theaters are dropping off by the 3rd or 4th week - is your local theater(s) still going strong? If going into the second month you are not losing show times during the weekend evenings you are in good shape. Once a film drops to a daily mid-afternoon time slot there is not much hope, because from one poor time slot per day it is unlikely to stay out of the bottom spots in the theater's weekend box office.

Theaters are businesses. It is not they "don't want" to play Christian film, but there needs to be some confidence that there is an audience. Once the film is in play, the audience will drive how long it plays. If you can stay in the top 3-6 spots of a theater playing 15 films, your film is generally pretty safe.

Suppose your local theater has 14 screens, and is playing 15 or 16 films each weekend. If the following weekend has three big new releases scheduled, a decision must be made as to which films end to make space. This is why you don't want to be in the bottom several spots. If you can camp out in the top six or eight earning films, and the theater management knows that you're still out promoting the film, you are probably in good shape. In time, even the most popular films fade, and it will happen with yours as well, but with advance efforts and strong word of mouth shoot for a month at least, maybe two.

When you sign up for a particular movie website's updates, share a brief description of your ministry. Such a note shows that you're not just obsessed with one of the actors as a borderline stalker. The Christian film industry recognizes the value brought by local support, but knowing you have been involved in promoting Christian films, understand the business side of the industry, and have an established network gives you additional credibility.

Being able to plug into that network and demonstrate it can count even more - as in the online contests noted above.

Can you bring media attention to the movie? Cultivate relationships with area radio stations or newspapers so that when something potentially newsworthy comes up, they know who you are when you share it. Again the key is respect - share the idea with some supporting information, but not in a way that will offend them or give the impression you will be ticked off if they don't feel your story is worthy of the front page, color photo you might think it deserves. (Because you, of course, are an impartial observer!)

Finally, and potentially the most difficult, can you find someone to buy out shows. There is a very good reason this is one of the key elements on almost every movie website's page. That reason is... this is still a business (starting to see a trend?)

If you have an individual, business, or church, who is willing to purchase an entire showtime (or more) the financial risk drops significantly. Imagine a 250 seat theater sells out at $8 each - that is $2000 from the one showtime.

If it costs $3000 for the print and promotion of bringing the film to town, that means the one showtime covers 2/3 of the cost. If you can drum up support for three or four sold out shows, now you have a guaranteed $8000 theater run - if NOBODY else buys a single ticket. This is a nearly ideal situation, but it has not happened to us yet, and we are not holding our breath.

Don't focus on what isn't happening, focus on where God is showing up, on the enthusiasm of someone you just met, and the tears (or laughter) of crowds coming out of a theater without feeling their morals were just attacked for the previous 2 hours.

ACTION! What tools, connections, or resources has God ALREADY equipped you with to build a Regional Movie Ministry, or whatever other area He has called you to?

_____

_____

4 MINDSET IS CRITICAL

You've probably picked up on this by now, but the most effective mentality for this ministry is to think long term. Film after film, how can you build momentum for the big opening weekend, then capture that momentum for the next film in line. Don't get too bogged down in dollar numbers or duration of theater runs, but instead see if you are building your subscriber lists with people who are really interested and actively involved.

The people who contact you - excited about helping - are your greatest assets. You will have many people signup for the emails, who may never open one. That's part of the game. Pay attention to the people who forward your emails and ask questions, because these people are the ones who are going to help grow the ministry, and encourage you when you need it. (It is still ministry, so there will definitely be times you need encouragement whether you are willing to admit it or not.)

Yes, this chapter is short. I strongly believe this mindset is the difference between your efforts being embraced by the churches, groups, and individuals in your area, or people diving for cover when they see you pull into their parking lots!

A long term mindset willing to look for where God is moving, soaking up that encouragement, and moving forward for His glory is the greatest thing you can cultivate in your life, not just in a Regional Movie Ministry, but for everything you do for His Glory!

ACTION! Are you ready to step out and serve God in a ministry that has no guarantee of "success," and willing to see where He leads it rather than following "your plans."

_____

_____

_____

_____

5 DEFINE YOUR SCOPE

What films will you promote/support? That's easy - "Christian" - right? But what is a Christian film?

We learned pretty early on that there is a wide range of definition for what a Christian film is. For some, the term Christian only means "family friendly" - no swearing, sex, violence, or other offensive content. I don't care for this definition, because I think any definition of "Christian" which eliminates the Bible itself, is inaccurate. Mel Gibson's *The Passion of the Christ* was not family friendly, but it certainly opened eyes to what our Savior went through on the cross far more effectively than thousands of Sunday School flannelgraph lessons.

For others, the film's defining moment must be a clouds parting, sun beam shining, opening of a troubled heart to the Gospel of Jesus Christ, followed by a sudden resolution to all of life's problems. While I certainly am all for the Gospel being presented, it needs to fit, and sometimes this scene is forced into the film and is the most memorable scene - but in a bad way.

Our rough definition of a Christian film is one with a biblical message, ideally references the Bible as the message's source / worldview, and not just some generic feel-good morality.

Will some disagree? Yes. Have we been criticized for a film we supported? Yes. Will you? Yes. No matter where you draw the line, some will think you should have pushed harder on one, or avoided another. By welcoming the discussion, being open and honest with the content, and being consistent, most will give you grace over the disagreements.

You and your ministry team, will need to wrestle with this idea, and yes, it may be a struggle. We have passed on a couple films which, though not bad films, we didn't feel met our criteria. We try to learn about the films, and preview before we put ourselves on the line directly endorsing a film. Your ministry can maintain integrity by being open with what you know or don't know about the film.

You can inform your audience about an upcoming film, without actively endorsing it as one they 'must see.' Honesty is appreciated.

Remember your ministry is to build awareness and support of Christian films, but your focus is the awareness side. Once a church or individual is aware of a film, they can visit the film website, research it online, find out what other films the stars have been in, and whatever other investigation they would like before determining the level of support they are willing to commit to.

How do you do this? There are any number of options, but we will look at a number of them in the coming chapters - use those you are most comfortable with to start, and grow into the others.

6 TOOLS OF THE TRADE
(IF ALL YOU HAVE IS A HAMMER…)

A. Email

In building your RMM, you want to steadily reach more individuals and groups with the same or less work. Email is a great way to do this, and an email marketing program makes it even more powerful, easier, and with better SPAM law protection.

Before we go further, let's affirm that yes, a personal invitation is the best way to invite anyone to anything. Once they are on board, however, your goal is to build an audience who do not need an in-person or even a phone call every time to know and share future opportunities. You want an audience who will read your email, and start inviting their friends, family, and circles of influence to join them at the theater. At this point, your ministry's effectiveness will start to take off, because it is no longer about you, your contacts, or your effort, but a collective network.

You might want to start with just a group email list in your email program. This allows you to send one email and know it hit everybody interested, rather than having to individually address or add individual addresses for each person.

The downside to this approach is that as your list grows, it becomes more work. You must manually add people to the list. You will get emails bounced that you will have to delete or change, and anyone who gets a new address MIGHT remember to tell you, and then you have to change it. More likely you'll end up needing to periodically review bounced emails and contacting the person (if possible) about their new address.

Further, this approach leaves you at risk for SPAM complaints, as there is no automatic way for people to opt-out of your list, or, for that matter, an easy way to track and confirm their desire to opt-in without your meticulous, perfect recordkeeping.

B. Email Marketing

Don't get bent out of shape over the idea of "E-mail Marketing" – you are completely in control of what you send out, and to who. The e-mail marketing programs simply allow you to provide an easy way for subscribers to sign up for your list(s), control their preferences of what lists they want to be on (allowing you to be as specific or general as you want!), and makes it easy for you to send out your messages.

There are also layout templates available which will allow you to add images, captions, etc far easier than you can within most email programs.

There is a cost involved, and that would need to be considered. Once your list grows beyond 50 or 100, however, there is also a cost involved for your time with ongoing list maintenance.

I made the switch to email marketing in 2008 with my men's event newsletter, and it was without a doubt one of the greatest investments I've made. Once set up, you can easily generate other email lists for various purposes, saving additional time. In my case, a month after getting set up, I was asked to lead the local team for a Promise Keepers men's conference, so there were lists for the leadership team, volunteers, and other groups as the year went on.

One of the most well known providers of e-mail marketing is Constant Contact.

Since 2008, I've used and recommend, Potter's E-Marketer. It is a central Illinois company owned by a man who is active in his church, publishes the area Christian yellow pages, and with whom I've worked together on a regional men's publication, SIXTH DAY MAGAZINE.

Potter's eMarketer   www.pottersemarketer.com

Constant Contact   www.constantcontact.com

There are of course many others, but these are the two that I've used (Potter's) or fairly familiar with through knowing others who use them. Just be intentional in investigating costs and budget accordingly. Is the cost driven by the number of emails or the size of your list. If the size of your list, as you reach the next threshold of cost, are you better off to pay more or to review your list and remove some of the inactive members? There are pros and cons to both sides, so consider the long term when signing up.

Another thing to remember about Email Marketing. A campaign sent to 400 people is NOT... repeat... NOT read by 400 people, or probably even 300. This is a shock to a lot of people when they first have access to the additional reporting and tracking tools of email marketing. A successful campaign may only be opened by 30-35% of recipients. *Gasp*

That's right, not everyone is online the second your email arrives for them to put everything else on hold until they read the latest breaking news you sent them. Sorry.

C. Social Networking

No one could have predicted the incredible growth of MySpace a few years back, or it's meltdown and current domination of Facebook. Some may want to skip the email route and just use Facebook.

I highly recommend setting up a Facebook page, but remember that the active users who have hundreds of friends also probably have thousands of posts/tweets / ??? hitting their accounts. For this reason, I think Facebook is a valuable tool, but not one that should replace emails that can hit a larger number of people, as there are who refuse to join Facebook for various reasons.

Facebook can also serve as an initial web presence. There may be benefits in time to have a full blown webpage, such as having the opportunity to set up movie-specific pages or address ongoing themes on a page that won't scroll down as new content is posted, but for a quick generation of awareness Facebook is tough to beat.

As noted before, when the movie *Hardflip* posted on Saturday,

February 18th, their plans to have Facebook posts determine their movie premiere, complete with cast party and giveaways, a quick note and update triggered a wave of support for Peoria that blew me away. On their initial post we recorded over 30 votes, and shot up to well over 100 before the weekend was over. That time was exciting, but led to great disappointment with a low theater turn out.

Twitter could also be used effectively, but I don't think most of the information shared about this ministry is so time-critical that Twitter is required. It might be a better tool for growing your audience through email subscriptions and likes.

In the end, social media comes down to where you are most effective and comfortable. If you already have a large Twitter following – leverage it. They all have their benefits and drawbacks, and using what you are comfortable with is going to be more beneficial than trying to hit them all and being overwhelmed and ineffective.

D. Website

We won't spend a lot of time on this one, because it largely is driven by your comfort level and available time. If you or a friend is willing to spend the time to learn and build a world class mind blowing website - that is fantastic. Do I think it is absolutely critical? Not really.

Rather than fancy graphics, keep in the forefront what you are doing, and why. Does it make sense to have a separate page set up for each film? Perhaps. Is there a benefit to keeping it all on one page so someone can just scroll down? Could be. There is not one right answer to this one. Talk to people who have been to the page, or ask people to look, and see what they say.

That was actually a pretty good idea, I think I'll do that myself! (see, we can all learn together).

One word of warning regarding embedded YouTube videos. At the end of the video, YouTube lists other videos they recommend, complete with small images from the videos. These are at their discretion, not yours, and we had an embarrassing moment when a friend called informing us that as their family finished watching a trailer on our website, several inappropriate images came up on the screen.

There are ways to filter this, but we don't need to go into that level of detail in this document. If you're uncertain on the specifics, check with your friend who knows all things technical, or don't worry about embedding the videos to your site, just provide links to the movie's direct website.

Remember your goal is NOT to replace the movie's site, but to provide one place for people within your region to get news and local information. The movie website likely has a higher budget than you for web design, and people understand that, so don't feel you must "keep up."

What can YOUR local website do better than the official movie page?

Here are a few ideas:

1. Provide quick and easy local theater information

This may define your "region" if you don't want to follow 30 theaters. The more rural an area, the wider a radius may be supportable. ALWAYS include a note to confirm with local theaters the showtimes, as they are subject to change.

2. Local connections to films

What If... director Dallas Jenkins's mother is from the small town of Manito, Illinois. In a bus station scene in the movie shot in a bus station, several cities are mentioned - including Manito. How about interesting cameos in the film? These little nuggets of information can be fun for people to watch for. For *What If...* we even set up a trivia contest that people could download from our website, submit their answers, and win some fabulous prizes.

3. Provide a local name and face to the Christian film industry

Most people will never meet Stephen or Alex Kendrick. Many churches don't know where to start to get a movie license for their church event. You have the opportunity to provide information to people about Christian films. As you learn about resources, make them available to others. Don't be insecure about sharing other websites or email lists. If someone wants more information about a Christian film, help them find whatever they need. Keep in mind people are the key to your ministry. How can you work together and in the process BOTH be more effective?

ACTION! With which of these tools are you already comfortable? How are you going to use them?

Were some of these ideas intimidating due to lack of experience, knowledge, or resources?

Don't avoid them forever just because YOU aren't familiar with them, it might be a great opportunity to grow your ministry team by finding someone to help out in that area!

_____

_____

_____

_____

_____

7 TAKE ME TO YOUR LEADERS (PRE-RELEASE SCREENINGS)

When available, these are a great way to get Christian leaders' support for a film. Depending on the movie, there will be different options available. For our first two movies, we were sent a screener DVD with which to host our own advanced screenings. Line up a church – preferably one with a pastor or several key leaders who support your movie efforts – and line up a date on which to show the movie there. Invite area leaders or key influencers to join you.

Early on, you will likely need to explain what you are doing, as many people aren't used to going to a church to view a film weeks or months from theaters - they may even ask if it is legal!

Explain that you are trying to provide them an opportunity to view the film so they can tell others first-hand what they thought of it. Emphasize at the screening that the intent is not for them to watch the film for free and then not go. Use the free advanced screening to encourage them to bring friends to the theater.

Some groups encourage these for "Pastors only," but our experience has been that often pastors can't make it, but other key leaders can. The key is to build buzz, and if 2 or 3 Sunday School teachers are more likely to share with various classes than a pastor to promote it from the pulpit, then accept that. Bottom line is that you want the people there who will tell others. More recently a couple films have begun referring to these as "Influencer Screenings" - a much better name in my opinion.

If you can afford it, have a drawing at the advanced screening for a Dinner & Movie, and then mention (good naturedly, please) that since that couple is going for free, they could pay to bring some friends.

This is also a chance to share about your ministry, upcoming movie trailers, and provide a sheet with upcoming Christian movie information. These sheets can be a reminder to people to visit your website later. Always provide a clear opportunity for people to sign up for your newsletters at these (and any) events you host, organize, or attend.

These are opportunities for your ministry to be positioned as the local "go to" place for Christian movies. Look at each interaction as a chance to connect with new people and grow your audience, which helps the next film effort.

A final note on the advanced screenings is to partner with other groups as possible. If the film has a natural connection to an area ministry, seek to partner with them. Offer them a display table at no cost, and ask them to share news about the movie and your efforts with their network of supporters or mailing list.

Note that these are related to advanced screenings which your ministry hosts. ALWAYS make sure to understand what the limitations and expectations are. You don't want 37 advanced screenings and then nobody at opening weekend. You may want to consider geography, hosting screenings in different areas of town or surrounding communities. Having options on different nights or times may also help you fit more people's schedules.

When the advanced screenings are hosted by the individual films or their extended marketing team, remember it is THEIR screening. They are in charge and responsible for details. Respect their specific purpose - to promote the movie which is paying for the evening. This is not the time to heavily promote another movie, and NEVER at the expense of the featured movie. This is, however a good opportunity to connect with attendees who heard of the film screening but never heard of you.

Offer to assist as needed, ask what would be acceptable to share or have available, but remember to keep the focus on the featured film for that night and the hosts, not your ministry. If you are offended because you requested a 3-table display and were rejected... get over it, pray about why you were there and why you are doing this ministry, and support the film. Remember it takes time to build trust. If the first time you ask for a table and display and a chance to talk to the attendees and... you come across as a pushy salesperson for your efforts, which is not the reason for the event.

If your town / region has multiple theaters and you are attending an event or movie at one, be diligent about not promoting something at their competition. If you have a display board, this is as simple as taking materials off which are exclusively at other theaters. People who come to your website can still learn about it, but you want each theater to understand you are on their team, and not working with someone down the street. The theaters will benefit financially from the film's success far more than your organization ever will, but you want them on your side as you work together for mutual benefit.

When looking to schedule an advanced screening night at a theater for one film we sponsored, we could not get a response back from the national management of the chain where the film will be playing. We talked with another, independent, theater, and had a date set in a couple days. Ideally, the advance screening and the theater run would be at the same theater, however in this situation we were running out of time.

The important thing is to make sure both theaters fully understand the situation. Consistent support over time, with unquestioned integrity. If this sounds like a broken record, it is meant to, because it is that important.

ACTION! Beyond the general mailing list, start a list of Influencers (not just Pastors) to invite to special events. It is not that they are "better" than others, but their influence and endorsement can build a crowd far better than someone who might go, enjoy it, and not tell anyone.

_____

_____

8 DINNER & MOVIES & PARTNERSHIPS (FOOD, FILMS, & FRIENDS)

As *What If...* approached its second month in the theaters, we decided to get a group together and see it a second time. It was during this meal of laughter and celebration that led to hosting similar gatherings for upcoming films on their opening weekends.

We choose a restaurant or other host site for dinner, and while people are eating we share news about the ministry, movie updates, and trailers for upcoming films. We also try to have some giveaways related to the movies or door prizes. These don't have to be expensive, and while I doubt anyone comes for these bonuses, they are an extra something over just a movie.

For example, for Seven Days in Utopia we gave each person at dinner two golf balls, each marked with SFT (See.. Feel... Trust) – see the movie or read the book *Golf's Sacred Journey* to understand why. It was a reminder of the movie's message for our supporters, and the second golf ball was to give away to someone else after the movie.

For more on the idea of touchstones, or Spiritual souvenirs, visit www.MenofAIM.org/touchstones

Door prizes or touchstones don't have to be expensive. You're already buying a group of tickets from a theater – ask if they would provide a couple concessions gift cards or a free popcorn (driving drink sales). If you're going to a restaurant with a large group, ask the manager when making the reservations if they would be willing to toss in a gift card or free dessert card for a future visit.

Regarding location, we've used three restaurants and two radio stations. We had one scheduled for a church but a miscommunication led to a last minute transition to a restaurant down the street. Ideally there would be a room large enough for your crowd plus space for ministry materials, an adequate A/V system, and access to get things set up and torn down in time to relax and enjoy the evening yourself.

An advantage of a church location is hopefully their hosting will create engagement in the event and promotion with their leaders and sister church. Pastoral buy-in for your ministry is a great path to growth.

If you can, set up the night before, and have volunteers lined up to help take stuff down afterwards. Provide time for dinner, discussion, and travel to the theater without speeding tickets (yes, that is the voice of experience).

For pricing, try to keep it affordable but cover your costs. There is no point hosting an event where more people is more loss, unless you have supporters willing to make up the difference (or more).

Include both dinner and the movie ticket in your pricing, and then have the movie tickets bought in advance so your guests can bypass the line and avoid any risk of the show selling out halfway through your group. The final cost will be largely dependent on the dinner selection. Most of ours have been priced at $20, but one was bumped up to $25 and involved an all-you-can-eat family style dinner.

Remember your purpose as you define the price point. Higher prices will cost too much for some couples/families, so keep in mind if you are looking at the night as a cost-neutral get together or a fund raiser. Our approach has been we'd rather keep the Dinner & Movie nights as cost neutral, and build support through people directly supporting the ministry.

As discussed with the advanced screenings, consider contacting area ministries whose mission aligns with the film. For example, for the Dinner & Movie for *October Baby*, a movie about the adopted survivor of a failed abortion, we had ministry tables set up for two local pro-life ministries to share materials.

The only limitation in this case is to determine the amount of space you have and the timing, since you will want the partnering ministries to share about their ministry with the attendees. While you are promoting a movie, they are ministering to people on a daily basis. Honor them for their time and participation.

Another change we have recently implemented with the increase in the number of films, are informal Dinner & Movies. Instead of the full blown A/V set up and sharing trailers, we just meet as a group at an area restaurant and people order/pay for their own food. This way we don't try to meet every person's taste or budget, and our only advance planning needs are reservations and purchasing movie tickets. Rather than a slideshow of news, we print out a sheet summarizing highlighting upcoming dates or other news.

Mix it up to see what works, and what doesn't, in your area. We're still trying new things ourselves. Don't get into a rut, and make sure you're having fun in the process.

ACTION! What churches, businesses, or restaurants near your area theaters might be interested in a Dinner & Movie?

What ministries in town do you already know? What ministries have you never even heard of? (Trick question - you don't know them yet!)

What steps will you take to learn about the full ministry picture, so when a film comes out a Dinner & Movie is a natural partnership?

_____

_____

_____

9 CHURCH RELATIONS
(PEST-FREE NETWORKING)

Though last, this is far from least. In fact, it may be the most important element working for (or against) you moving forward.

Building a base of supportive churches for your RMM will reap great benefits. We have several churches that we know with a couple phone calls or emails we can line up an advanced screening, AND know they will help build a crowd. Knowing in advance which churches are willing to put up posters, use bulletin inserts, or utilize PowerPoint slides allow you to cover their needs quickly. The saved time can then be spent networking with new churches, groups, and individuals.

The biggest item to consider in building these networks comes from Mrs. Aretha Franklin herself - RESPECT.

Always respect the church and pastor's time. They have many groups battling for limited space, time, and other resources.

It is this very reason we believe established RMM's are a crucial ongoing communication tool for promoting Christian films than an individual or team driven by one particular film or project.

The first few times (or more) you drop in at a church to share about a Christian film, they may be a bit wary, because they see you as a salesperson not a ministry. Churches are used to being hit up with the classic, "Here's a great film (or Bible study, or resource, or book) that you simply <u>must</u> put in the hands of your congregation."

Over time, if you are respectful of the church's time and resources, eventually a particular movie you share may strike a chord with them. Different churches will respond to different films - just like different people. Once churches recognize your intent truly is to inform and assist - NOT sell them on a specific film, trust will build.

The churches may become a great resource to you, as they may hear of a film and let you know about it. Your ongoing ministry and their growing awareness of the impact of film can allow you to be their first contact if they decide to host a movie screening. Since they trust you, there is a good chance they would allow you to set up a ministry table at their movie night.

That's also the perfect situation for you - where better to sign up people for communications about Christian films than at the screening of another Christian film? The host church may also be more open to your sharing your vision and mission - with their endorsement!

ACTION! Are you ready to sacrifice the short term, for the long?

10 TOOLS & RESOURCES
(WHY REINVENT THE WHEEL?)

A number of different resources will be available for download at www.richgerberding.com/rmm. There is nothing magic about them, but are either blank forms for use in a format I have found helpful (by all means, set up your own format in whatever way helps you the most!) Thanks for your support of our effort, and hopefully your willingness to launch a regional ministry of your own wherever you are located.

PLEASE let us know if you start a similar ministry - we plan to track and watch these groups grow across the nation, and maybe the world. This way people moving to a new area can look to see if there is a group already in place in their new area.

You can also join our mailing list at www.richgerberding.com/rmm

We are not looking to create an empire, or collect fees by making this a "franchise." If you like our approach and want to put your efforts under a similar name like "Sarasota Christian Movie Central" - that's great, but it's about building support, not what name is on individual groups.

Of course, if you do feel led to support our ministry financially as a regular supporter or a special gift, we are humbled and thankful.

In time, it will also be beneficial as the number of groups grow to see when we start "bumping into" one another - not necessarily a bad thing as it allows each group to have greater focus on a smaller area. Let's not get territorial - let's focus on building the Kingdom, not egos!

We have set up a starter template of some key information that is helpful as you move forward. Which lists are helpful will depend on your area of focus (theatrical releases, church or independent screenings, etc.) Download the Excel file at www.richgerberding.com/rmm

Please note the first several are not filled out for your area, but templates for compiling the information as you build your network.

    A. List of Church Contacts

    B. Venues / Options

    C. Media Contact List

    D. Online Promotion Opportunities

    E. Some Key Websites / Groups / Resources to get started

    F. Movies Licensing Sites (always subject to Change)

What will this ministry (or ministries) look like in a year? Two years? Ten? We don't know - but God does, and we look forward to serving Him alongside you!

ABOUT THE AUTHOR

Rich Gerberding is the ministry director of Men of AIM, a regional men's ministry based in Peoria, Illinois. He has worked with many ministries to promote or organize events, including Man in the Mirror and Promise Keepers. He lives in the Heart of Illinois with his wife and teen-age son. In addition to men's ministry and films, he is known for his "unique sense of rare humor" and for an over-the-top appetite for steak and bacon.

www.richgerberding.com
Twitter   @Gerberding
www.facebook.com/richgerberding

For more about Regional Movie Ministries

www.richgerberding.com/rmm
www.facebook.com/regmoviemin

For more information about Men of AIM:

www.MenofAIM.org
www.facebook.com/menofaim

For more about "our" Regional Movie Ministry:
Heart of Illinois Christian Movie Central

www.menofaim.org/movies
www.facebook.com/hoicmc

Finally, and far less importantly, if you just love steak and/or bacon:

www.carnediem.com
www.cafepress.com/menofaim
Shirts, mouse pads, other products -
all sales support the ministries of Men of AIM

Psst...The book is over. Now it's time to do something.

Organize a group to a movie.

Share this book with a friend.

Take a first step - *any* step!

Do SOMETHING. Take ACTION. PRAY continuously.

Thanks for your time and interest!

Rich

07082014